THE YOUNG SPORTSMAN'S GUIDE TO
FRESH WATER FISHING

THE YOUNG SPORTSMAN'S LIBRARY

THE
YOUNG SPORTSMAN'S GUIDE
TO
FRESH WATER
FISHING

by

Ray Ovington

THOMAS NELSON & SONS

Edinburgh   NEW YORK   *Toronto*

THIRD PRINTING, AUGUST 1963

© *1961, by Thomas Nelson & Sons*

Library of Congress Catalog Card No.: 61-8359

MANUFACTURED IN THE UNITED STATES OF AMERICA

Acknowledgments

No matter how much a man can learn about fishing, it is at best only a beginning. This book may be the beginning of basic knowledge and information about one of the greatest sports in the world. It does not try to contain all the writer knows about fishing, but it does attempt to place in the hands of the beginner the beginnings. From there he can progress by reading and by doing.

Here, we try to put the right tackle in your hands, show you how to use it and then send you forth to the waterside. From there on in you are on your own.

The way to learn how to fish is to fish!

So that you will not go there without adequate guidance, the author has called on a number of his friends in the fields of making, selling, and using fishing gear of all kinds. Many have been guides, outfitters, backwoodsmen, sophisticated big-city anglers, and angling writers. Here are some of the people who helped make this book possible: Jim Deren of the Angler's Roost, Chrysler Bldg., NYC; Irv Kay and Arthur Mills, William Mills and Sons, NYC; Bob Zwirz, Angler's Cove, 3rd Ave. and 32nd St., NYC; editor and publisher, Sheldon Shane of *Fishing World Magazine,* 50 West 57th St., NYC; Ted Hecht, editor of the Stanco Magazine Sports Library, NYC; Bob Stewart, sports editor of the *New York World-Telegram and Sun;* and the many anglers known and unknown the author has met on the lakes and streams of the world.

The author wishes to thank the publishers of his two books, *How To Take Trout,* Little, Brown and Co., and *Spinning In America,* the Stackpole Co., for the use of material and photos that appeared first in these volumes. Also thanks go to the *Pennsylvania Angler* magazine, *Field and Stream, Sports Afield, Hunting and Fishing, Outdoors, Think, Travel, Fresh and Salt Water Fishing* for material and photos that first appeared in those publications. Additional thanks to the publishers of the *World-Telegram and Sun* for material used from my daily column.

Table of Contents

Chapter I

The Fun of
Fresh Water Fishing

To attempt to describe the fun of fresh water fishing would take a full lifetime, for fishing is a lifetime of fun, no matter where you fish, how you fish, or what tackle or techniques you use.

There are three basic pleasures in fishing. One is that you have the opportunity to engage in a sport where there are no constants such as are found in such sports as tennis, golf, or any of the team games. In these the boundaries are all prescribed. There are no boundaries in fishing. Water, weather, general conditions are never the same, nor are the types and kinds of water ever alike. We haven't even mentioned the varieties of fish and their many changes of habit, mood, feeding, and striking abilities. Another enjoyable part of fishing is that it gets a fellow out in the open, away from the cities, away from civilization with all its many restrictions. When a man fishes, he is his own boss and is answerable only to Mother Nature. She, by the way, is not a bad gal to know, for she has many secrets. Yet another fun aspect of fishing is the ownership of tackle and the ability to choose the right outfit, lure, and technique for the particular situation at hand. These are the fishing adventures, whether they be just a jaunt to the neighborhood lake, or a trek into the far wilderness. Fishing, you will find, is full of wonderful surprises.

In this book the author has presented a great deal of information which can be the springboard for further knowing-by-fishing. It is a generalized roundup of some of the many tricks and kinks he has learned from his father and other guides,

friends, and strangers on the lake and stream. No one book will ever tell enough. If this one gets you started on the road to fishing fun, it will have served its purpose.

Fishing has a great history and heritage into which you are moving. Many millions before you have found the tight line thrilling. Once you start you will have joined the brotherhood.

From time immemorial, man has fished and hunted, first for food, then, gradually, his means of livelihood turned into a great sport. Fly fishing started before the birth of Christ when men and women tied bits of feathers to crude hooks and the fish came up to them. Since then anglers have been perfecting their lures, tackle, and techniques in order to better the game of fun

with fish. Many great statesmen have been anglers and many a
philosopher has gained the peace he has needed through a day
of fishing and thinking.

Izaak Walton is known as the father of fishing. Get a copy
of his book; in fact, go to your library and look up some of the
books suggested in the Bibliography. You'll find good reading
here, lots of helpful hints, stories of fishing from all over the
world. More books have been written on the pleasures of angling
than all other sports combined. Read about fishing when you
cannot go fishing because of season, study, or work.

Fishing tackle developed when man first coiled a rope,
tied a hook to the end of it, and threw it into the water. First,

single-action reels were developed and attached to poles. Then, years later someone developed the revolving-spool reel that has not changed basically since. Spinning, that is fishing with a reel with a stationary spool, then came along as the latest, and some consider the best, development in fishing's history.

Rods, lines, nets, boots, waders, tackle boxes, and a host of gadgets have come along to aid further in the fun of fishing.

With all of this, the fish haven't changed a bit. They are as dumb as they ever were, despite the fact that many anglers like to attribute great craftiness to them as an excuse for an empty creel.

It just is not so. There still remains the trick of discovering just how a fish lives, what he feeds on and when and why. As you learn that a fish merely does what comes naturally to him, and can find out ways to appeal to his instincts, then you are well on the way to joining the 10 per cent of the fishermen who catch 90 per cent of the fish. This may take you a lifetime, but the fun along the way will be well worth it. You will find that you will at first want to catch all the fish you can legally. Later on, as you gain the respect of Mother Nature and learn her secrets, you will, it is hoped, not divulge her secrets, nor take advantage of her. Usually the man who becomes a good fisherman becomes interested in the most sporting way to catch fish rather than concentrating on the ways to catch the most fish all the time.

You'll get to know a great many fishermen but few real sportsmen. There is a difference, believe me. It is hoped that there is a rod and gun club near your home and that you will introduce yourself and become a member. Perhaps it will be necessary to round up a few of your friends and form a club so that you can get together in fun sessions to discuss tackle, help each other select good fishing outfits, and instruct newcomers to the sport. Make sure that sportsmanship is the password with every member especially as it applies to obeying the laws of your state and club. These laws are made for good reason and that is the conservation of our wildlife. Our states have excellent conservation departments which are supported by your fishing-and hunting-license money. They need all the cooperation they can muster from all sportsmen. If you bear in mind that the game poacher is a real thief, you will realize the need for helping the warden whenever possible.

We hope that your father is a fisherman too, and that he will help you to select the proper kind of equipment necessary for the fishing you will be doing first, right in your immediate area. If he is not a fisherman, once you get a start and have caught your first few fish, why not talk him into joining you. It will do him good, get his mind off business, and chances are he'll help you get new gear when you need it.

If you have a younger brother, take him along and show him the way to fish.

All fishing is different and offers its particular thrills. When you are able to cast a dainty dry fly over a glassy trout pool of a mountain stream and make the trout come up and take it, there is a sensation that will be long remembered. The bass that bursts from beneath the lily pad to pounce on your plug will make you jump a bit in response. Even the little sunfish that grabs a worm dangled over the end of the dock can be

a lot of fun. Believe it or not, many of the world's most sophisticated anglers go panfishing. They find a special thrill even though they are used to fighting the great salt water fish.

Certainly the first time you view an Atlantic salmon jumping over a twelve-foot waterfall, you will wonder what that fish can do to your frail fly rod. It is all fun, every minute of it.

Like all enterprises, there is a right way and a wrong way to do things. Before you even think of going to a stream or lake get to know the tackle you have so that you can operate it almost without thinking. The time spent on the stream or lake is for fishing fun, not tackle learning. A backlash, a tangled line, the wrong knot or rig can quickly end a good day of fishing. Think these things out in advance and keep your tackle in order at all times.

It is fun to learn all there is to know about the fish in your vicinity. Some of this information can come from books, but the most important things will come through your eyes. The smart outdoorsman uses his eyes constantly and learns to find out the ways of the wild through experience.

In the chapters that follow we introduce you to the three basic types of tackle and their uses, advantages, and disadvantages under specific conditions and for particular fish. We also delve briefly into the various species of fish, so that you can get an idea of just which ones you are interested in and which are available close to home. However, it is a good plan to know a little about all of them, for you never know when you will be travelling into strange country. There is good fishing everywhere in our great country, and thanks to increased conservation efforts, it is becoming better and better even near our biggest cities.

You will read many books whose authors tell you how difficult it is to learn to handle tackle and become an expert fisherman. In some cases these authors have the idea that to make the sport seem difficult will arouse interest.

Learning to operate modern tackle is not difficult. A fairly responsive person can learn to make the usual casts in a very few hours. Learning the technique of properly wading a trout stream may take a little longer, and certainly the special effects can only be learned by long experience, developed along the way from necessity.

At first we are all awkward in learning to tie a knot, make a cast, or wade a stream, just as we are the first time we try to paddle a canoe or row a boat. That all passes quickly

and then you are free to really enjoy your days and nights on the water. Now, let's go fishing!

Chapter II

The Most Popular
Fresh Water Sport Fish

There are many species of fresh water fish in North America. Listed here are only a few of the most popular, simply because they have won their place in anglers' hearts ever since this land was first discovered. What constitutes game fish is a debatable point in that so many of the lesser fish have become game fish since light tackle has become popular. Even the catfish is a gamey fish taken on light gear. Sport means fun, so actually any fish that provides fun is a game or sport fish, so all of them qualify in one way or another. Latin names accompany the brief descriptions so that you can research any one of them further.

We have written a bit about each, preferring not to go too deeply into the methods and techniques for catching them as this material is farther along in the book under separate chapters.

There are so many popular names given to fish that the Latin identification with the picture was felt to be necessary.

Brook Trout *(Salvelinus fontinalis)*

The brook trout is a native of the eastern states and a favorite of fishermen. All types of fresh water tackle are used, but fly fishing can be the most exciting. Ultralight spinning gear is also heartily recommended.

The brook trout is really a char, not a member of the salmon family. Its nearest relatives are the lake trout and the Dolly Varden trout of the West.

The average size varies with the waters and conditions, but the biggest practical weight is from two to four pounds. The majority of fish creeled are usually under a pound unless taken from deep lakes or from seldom-fished wilderness waters. The biggest on record weighed 14¼ pounds.

Their color is brilliant with dark and light green-brown worm-like markings on the back, shading into blue-green on the sides to offset the gold, blue, and white spots. The fins are orange-red marked with a black and white stripe. The tail is colored the same and is square in shape, which gives this trout its other name of squaretail. They feed on minnows, flies, and bugs in lake and stream.

Rainbow Trout *(Salmo gairdnerii)*

All the species of true salmon-trout such as the rainbow, steelhead, cutthroat, and the mountain trout are fast-water fish, brilliantly colored. The rainbow has a wide pink-red stripe down its side, set off by small black spots. It is colored blue-green on its back and yellow-pink on its belly. It is a hard fighter, taking to the air in spectacular leaps when hooked, as opposed to the general body-rolling fight of the brook or brown trout. It demands cold fast streams where there is plenty of oxygen and it is as choosy as the brook trout when it comes to stream conditions.

Originally the rainbow was only found in western streams, particularly the mountain watersheds leading to the Pacific Coast. Now, thanks to improved conservation and restocking, they are found in streams and lakes all across the northern trout belt from Washington to Maine. They spawn in the spring and when possible reside in deep lakes and return to the ocean to grow big and fat. They feed on all kinds of minnows, crayfish, insects, and baby fish of their own kind and seem to have an insatiable appetite.

Brown Trout *(Salmo trutta)*

The brown trout is not a native American. It was introduced in America in 1880 by Von Behr from German stock and has retained the name of German brown ever since. While not as beautifully marked as our eastern brook, it is nonetheless a prize catch. All types of fresh water tackle are employed in lake and stream and the brown puts up a good fight, running a bit larger in size than some of the other trouts. The biggest brown ever taken weighed 39 pounds. They average in a good stream from one to four pounds, and heavier in big deep lakes.

The brown trout is a fly-fishing favorite, for it stays out in midstream, taking flies from the surface during hatches of insects. It is a much more avid open-water feeder than either the rainbow or the brook. Its ability to stand warmer water temperatures has made the brown the lifesaver of trout fishing in waters no longer suitable for brook or rainbow trout.

The basic color is brownish green with prominent black spots, some with reddish centers. The fins are plain, not barred like the brook trout. In the larger sizes, their heads grow quite large and their lower jaw begins to grow a hook. They are very cannibalistic and large ones should be taken from the streams whenever caught. They are a very scary trout and particularly selective when feeding on hatching insects.

They, like the brook trout, spawn in the fall months ascending from ponds and lakes into the high tributary streams. At this time they are voracious feeders, killing everything from tiny insects to other trout and fish almost half their size.

The salmons: Atlantic, landlocked, and Pacific

We have grouped all the salmons in one section because our purpose here is merely to give you a general introduction to them.

The Atlantic salmon, *Salmo salar,* is found in upper Maine, and the eastern Canadian provinces. They grow to a size of forty pounds, averaging from fifteen to twenty pounds. They are caught with fly tackle only in streams from June until October. Known as the "leaper" the Atlantic puts up the greatest fight of any of the species.

The landlocked salmon or ouananiche, *Salmo salar sebago,* is limited to northeastern North America and is mainly a lake fish ascending feeder streams to spawn. Its fight is not as spectacular as the Atlantic, nor does it grow as large, averaging from four to six pounds. When the ice melts in the spring, fly and spin fishermen take them readily, but as soon as the water warms up they go to the depths of the lakes and can then be taken only by deep trolling.

There are several species of Pacific salmon and we will deal with them only generally. They ascend the streams from the ocean and can be taken on spoons at the mouths of rivers and creeks and with flies and lures upstream. Some of them grow to eighty pounds and can put up quite a battle.

The tackle for these big fish is similar to light boat and surf tackle used in striped-bass fishing and the method is trolling, with spoons and spinners. The landlocked salmon and Atlantic are caught mainly with fly and spinning gear using light lures and flies.

Steelhead Trout *(Salmo gairdnerii)*
Cutthroat *(Salmo clarkii)*
and Mountain Trouts

The steelhead trout of British Columbia, Washington, Oregon, and California is similar in fighting ability to the Atlantic salmon, but its feeding habits are quite different. The steelhead follows the salmon upstream and eats the eggs dropped by them. It also feeds on small fish and insects, so it offers a variety of ways to angle for it. It is very similar to the salmon in markings, although it is generally a much slimmer fish. It leaps wildly when hooked. Size varies from three to thirty pounds and can be caught during the runs which occur several times each season. This is the fish most often confused with the rainbow. In fact many scientists now class it as a rainbow trout, the differences being slight. Many of the rainbows imported to the East have steelhead bloodlines. The steelhead is an ocean fish ascending the streams; this separates him from the rainbow whose spawning habits are different.

The cutthroat is a close relative of the rainbow and steelhead and has the characteristic reddish coloration behind and below the gills. It does not grow to as large as the steelhead, generally running from three to six pounds but lacks nothing in its fighting spirit. They are found in lakes and streams and are similar in habits to the rainbow, and for some reason can stand warmer lake temperatures than the rainbow. Despite this fact they have not been successfully transplanted from their native West Coast and intermountain domain.

The golden and other high-altitude trout, the most brilliantly colored trout of North America, are found only in the high Sierra Mountains of California. These fish are much smaller and found only in the mountain creeks and deep spring-fed lakes where the temperature remains cold all year long.

Smallmouth Black Bass *(Micropterus dolomieu)*

The smallmouth bass can be readily distinguished from the largemouth by the fact that the upper lip does not extend back of the eye. It is generally a slimmer fish than the largemouth and of a bronzier coloration, though quite often the two fish cannot be distinguished from one another from the color standpoint. The smallmouth is found in rivers and lakes in the northern states where the largemouth cannot live, although they overlap in most central states. While the smallmouth does not grow to as large as the largemouth, averaging from two to eight pounds, it makes up the difference in fighting ability, pound for pound putting up a more ferocious fight than any of the trouts. Both species take surface fly-rod bugs, underwater and surface spinning- and bait-casting plugs, depending on the conditions.

Depending on the location, bass are hooked from late spring to late fall. They are not a migrating fish like some of the trout, but hold to a specific location in a lake or stream and will guard their domain against all comers, including your lures. They can be easily provoked at times into striking almost any kind of lure that makes a disturbance in the water, coming out in a savage rush, hitting the lure, and tail dancing with it across the water. More often than not they will throw even the treble hooks unless the angler keeps just the right amount of tension on the line. The smallmouth is judged to be co-partner with the largemouth as America's favorite game fish.

Largemouth Bass *(Micropterus salmoides)*

The largemouth bass covers a larger area of the country than the smallmouth, being found from the tip of Florida all the way to the Canadian border. In the southern states it weighs from five to fifteen pounds, averaging in the North Country from three to seven pounds. It is distinguished technically from the smallmouth by the fact that the upper jaw extends to behind the eye. The markings and coloration are similar to the smallmouth, except that it has a pronounced grouping of green splotches along the lateral line. The largemouth is also broader and fatter than the smallmouth.

The largemouth is found mostly in lakes and slow backwater meadow streams, feeding on crayfish, minnows, flies, bugs, frogs, and mice. It is a voracious feeder, guarding its nest or locale with devilish killing instinct. The best lures are surface plugs, bugs, and flies when the water is calm; and underwater wounded-minnow plugs when trolled or cast underwater. Spinning, bait-casting, and fly gear are used for lure as well as bait fishing.

Both species spawn in the late spring and at that time they are most easily provoked by surface lures cast over the spawning beds. In some states, fishing for them at this season is illegal for conservation reasons. They are great fun to cast for at night either from the shore of the lake or from a boat drifted quietly along the coves and stream inlets.

Northern Pike *(Esox lucius)*

Found all over the world, the pike is known for its fanatical fighting ability. They are also popular because of their delicious flesh. In North America they do not live below the midstate range, paralleling the domain of the smallmouth bass. Deep, clear northern lakes and big inlet rivers are the favored haunts of the pike. They feed on small fish, mice, birds, and freshly hatched ducklings—anything that moves and looks like food. Bigger tackle is required than for bass, particularly the line and lure size. Underwater, diving, surface lures cast with either bait-casting or spin-casting equipment are the rule, for they seldom if ever take flies and bass bugs.

They are the smaller cousin of the muskellunge, but are none the less a gamey fighter. Their color is light greenish, blending into a bronze on the back, and peppered with bean-shaped darker spots. They average from two to fifteen pounds and are every inch a tough subsurface fighter, seldom leaping clear, but preferring to body roll and bulldog on the surface in an effort to shake the hook.

Their biggest trick, common to all the pikes, is to fight hard well out from the rod, relax, and swim with you as you reel them in and then at the last moment when they become frightened, explode right in your face, not stopping their wrangling even after they have been netted and brought into the boat. They have very sharp teeth and it is best to kill them immediately before they can do any damage.

Chain Pickerel *(Esox niger)*

Baby brother of the pike and musky, the chain pickerel is found in lakes and ponds all across the country from Florida up to and including the realm of the other two species. Every bit the fighter on light tackle, they offer more opportunities for anglers simply because they are more prevalent, living in lakes and waters unsuitable sometimes even for the basses. They feed on minnows, frogs, crayfish, and so forth.

Light spinning gear, fly rods, and bait-casting equipment can be used with smaller lures and bait for lake and pond fishing and the angler will get a thrill when he hooks one, because of their savagery.

In coloration they are light greenish-brown, blending to a white-yellow on the belly, but with the characteristic chain markings of darker color which extend almost the length of the body. They run from one to five pounds.

Quite often the best place to find them is in the high grass beds along the shore, or in the middle of the lake where shallows produce thick weed growth.

While not as active strikers as the bass, they can best be brought to action by patient and slow retrieve of the lure over their lair. They take some time to make up their minds to strike, but once they do they follow through with the urge. Like the pike and musky they pull the old stunt of coming in quite easily and then battling all at once for dear life.

Muskellunge (Esox masquinongy)

The largest, most ferocious of the pike family and undisputed game fish of America, the musky is all fresh water fish packed into one. Nothing is as fierce in its feeding habits as the musky. He grabs young ducklings from the surface and leaps up to grab birds off overhanging trees. He'll take on a big carp, or other lesser fish including bass and trout. Often thought of as the alligator of the freshwater, no fish or small animal is safe when he is around.

He is found in a few midwestern states but his main baliwick is the central Canadian provinces. New York State is his eastern limit and the best waters in the East are in the St. Lawrence River. They reach six feet in length and run from 60 to 80 pounds.

He demands good staunch bait-casting tackle. Lately, many anglers are using spinning gear on him, but the heavy lines needed plus the heavy baits require a tough outfit, especially when it comes time to set the hook hard and fast. The shorter stiffer bait-casting rod is found to be much superior to most spinning rods ordinarily used for bass.

The biggest muskies are taken by casting or trolling large bait fish that have been harnessed. They are allowed to swim as naturally as possible right into his lair. The musky often mouths the bait for five minutes or more, exasperating the angler into striking too soon and thus pulling the bait out of his mouth. Often you don't get a second chance, for muskies that are big are smart.

Yellow Perch *(Perca flavescens)*

It is difficult to determine which of the panfish is the most popular. Certainly the yellow perch is high on the list where it is found. Seldom going over a couple of pounds in weight, the yellow makes this up in spirit and numbers.

One of the prettiest of the panfish, with its orange tinted fins, its basic yellow color banded with vertical V-shaped bars down its dark brown-green sides and its shiny scales it is a fish rivaling the golden trout for art honors.

Found in almost every state of the Union, it is so prolific it hardly ever needs restocking in water pure enough to house it. It is the ideal panfish to start out with when learning to handle your tackle and getting used to the sport of fishing. Where there is one perch there is likely to be a whole mob of them, all eager to take your bait or flies with abandon, the school scattering a bit as one is brought to net, and then coming in again to join the fun and the race for the bait. While perch take flies at times and spinners also, they are more likely to go for worms on not-too-fancy gear, another reason they are so much fun for the beginner.

Look for perch in any slow meandering meadow stream, pond, or lake. Quite often you'll hit into a school of them while fishing for bass or crappie and they offer a colorful addition for your picture album and a treat for the dining-room table. Many anglers vote the yellow perch next to the walleyed pike for table taste.

Light gear is recommended when specifically fishing for perch. As with all panfish, ultralight spinning gear and light fly rod will suffice. There is no limit on perch, and thus, no limit on fun either.

Walleyed Pike *(Stizostedion vitreum)*

Here is a fish that is a combination of a perch and a pike. Known by many names such as walleye, walleye perch, pike perch, and in Canada, doré, this great table delicacy combines with a great amount of fighting spirit to offer one of the best combinations to be found in fresh water. While they are bony, their meat is sweet and delicious. They run in size from three pounds to seven or eight in unusual cases. Their color is a drab mixture between the perch and the pike and varies a great deal due to locale.

Catching them is a combination of simple perch fishing and more exacting pike angling. They are mostly bait feeders and are not taken as a rule on most lures. Stillfishing and slow trolling along the deep runs of the lake produce the most strikes. Bait-casting and spinning tackle may be employed. The fly rod is seldom ever used specifically for them. They will on occasion take shiny spoons and spinners especially when accompanied by a strip of pork rind or rubber imitation of it.

They will be lured quite often when trolling for bass or pike, and their weight will give your light tackle a good argument.

Walleyes range over most of the bass, musky, and pike areas of the country and are found in company with these species. They are much more abundant than the others and it seems that they can hardly be fished out, being heavy breeders and really tough fish, overcoming such handicaps as pollution. They like deep-water lakes and slow, deep streams. Even the muddiest water will take care of the walleye, a fact that has endeared him to thousands from coast to coast. Baked walleye is a delicacy not to be missed.

White Perch *(Morone americana)*

While classed as a perch, its habits are not at all similar to the yellow perch. This is more a school fish, surfacing in great bands at various times of the day. You can be fishing for any lake species and all of a sudden for no reason at all a school of whites will begin surfacing on the calm lake not far from the boat. In the early part of the year, the fish are small, but nonetheless eager to grab tiny spinners and buck-tail flies cast to the edge of the school. Their fight is tremendous even though it might take four of them to make a pound. In the late fall some of the schools will contain fish weighing almost two pounds. The bigger ones are usually not surfacing, preferring to remain down deep in the company of the trout and bass. Quite often while still fishing for either, the white perch will grab hold of your night crawler and offer quite a tussle. Not until you get the fish to the surface will you know that it is not a trout.

They are a silvery fish with fairly large scales and no distinguishing markings.

Ultralight spinning lures, spinners, and fly-rod bucktails with tinsel shanks are the best bet. A well-cast, small-size worm will also draw in the big ones. They hit quite hard and if present at all you will not have to wait long while still fishing for them. During the hot summer months seek them out near deep holes in the lake and spring holes or stream inlets.

Once in a while they will take dry flies from the surface. Quite often under specific conditions they will be found feeding off the surface in company with trout, but this is the exception.

Sunfish *(Family centrarchidae)*

All the lesser panfish, the sunfish, bluegill, green sunfish, shellcracker sunfish, and warmouth can be grouped together as some of the prettiest fish to be found in America. What they lack in weight and consequently in fighting ability they more than make up in looks. They rival many of the tropicals for real beauty and, as a matter of fact, many aquarium fanciers prefer them to many of the tropicals.

If you want to have fun with your very light tackle, especially your fly rod, go buy very light leaders and use the lightest fly rod or ultralight spinning rod you can find and then tie in very small hooks for bait or the smallest lures made.

These species are found all over the map in any water supply that is not badly polluted. Where one is found, a whole school will be nearby ready to close in once you lower the bait or flip the lure.

Comes the day you want to take a kid brother fishing, start him out on "sunnies" and you'll have another angler in the family very quickly. Often when teaching a youngster to learn to cast, the sunfish will take the fly whether you are ready for the strike or not. The most fun is dry fly fishing with your very light trout gear.

There is no limit on the number of panfish you can take, so you can fish for them until you fill a pail. They are meaty for their size and a little care in filleting them will offer a supper of some of the tastiest meat you have ever eaten. When all else fails and you want an hour or two of fishing fun, go for them at any time of the year and they'll be ready and waiting.

Shad *(Alosa sapidissima)*

The shad is similar in habits to the Atlantic salmon in that it migrates from the salt water in the spring where it cannot be taken on lure or bait, to the streams where it migrates to the spawning area far upstream. Only in fresh water will the shad strike a lure, for it, like the salmon, does not feed while on the "run."

Shad are found on both the Atlantic and the Pacific coasts and they run up the streams, remaining in the fresh water for a month or so. They range from two to five and eight pounds, the hen or roe shad outweighing the bucks by a pound or more. Shad roe, the eggs from the hen, are a well-known table delicacy.

They can be taken on light tackle whether it be the fly rod, ultralight spinning, or bait-casting gear. As they do not take bait of any kind, they can be enticed with small spinning lures, spinners, and even very small wet flies with tinsel on the hook shank. Often red and white beads strung on the hook shank will bring hefty strikes. They bite from annoyance or perhaps from a childhood urge, carried over from when they fed on small insects and tiny bait fish as they were growing up for the migration back to the sea.

Shad are a very bony fish, but this does not detract from their goodness at the table. There are many good recipes by which you can cook them well, dissolving the bones.

Care must be taken in hooking and playing shad for their mouths are exceptionally fragile, like their near cousin the herring. Play them gently but firmly and do not allow them to fight too long or the hook will wear away a hole and they will slip off. Horsing them in will not work well either, so try and strike a happy medium.

Chapter III

What Tackle?

Before detailing the various kinds of tackle, I want to strongly suggest to you to purchase the best tackle available. Cheap, badly built and designed tackle is a foolish investment. Inadequate gear is equally hard to use and often unsatisfactory. Fishing can be fun only when you are armed with the right equipment. You wouldn't play tennis with a bad racquet, nor would you attempt even nine holes of golf with ill-fitting and crudely made clubs.

Very good tackle is available today and the equipment pictured here is just that. You won't go wrong in taking this little book with you to the tackle store and selecting your

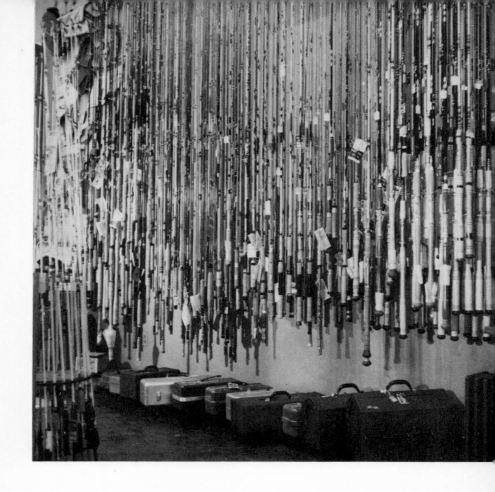

outfit from it. There are stores where you can obtain better prices than others. There are also many mail-order houses where good discounts can be had. There is no harm in buying name merchandise at the best price.

Before choosing the type of tackle you will be using, it is best to know the three basic types and their uses. From this description you can then go forth, make a choice of one or two and, perhaps, if you fish for many varieties of fish under a number of conditions, all three types will find their way into your collection.

While the three types and methods overlap to a degree, especially when used with bait, no one of them can be called universal. Some anglers have a distinct preference which has built up because of a certain dislike of the others. Some have come to one type after using all of them, the choice being one made over a long period of fishing in a certain preferred way.

Fly reels come in various sizes from light to heavy to accommodate any situation.

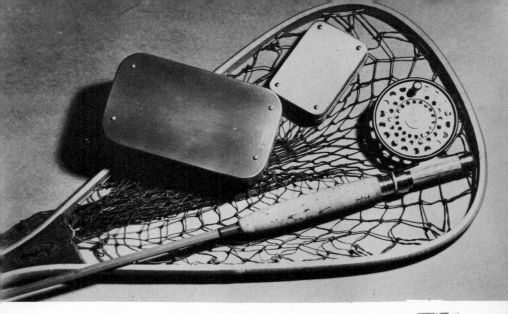

Fly-fishing equipment is used for casting very, very light artificial flies on delicate leaders a long distance from the angler. The rod comes in lengths from six to ten feet and is made of split bamboo or tubular glass fibers. The action is a wavy type, the line guides are many, to keep the line close to the rod so that the bend is under equal pressure. The close guides allow the line to be cast freely. Under certain conditions the line is shot through the guides in a cast which will be discussed later. The line is tapered so as to balance with the action of the rod. Some lines are double tapered from thin to thick to thin and come marked so that the right line can be bought for the right rod. This is what is known as matched or balanced tackle. The wrong line with the very best rod will render it almost useless, for it will cast poorly. The leaders, monofilament nylon, are tapered from heavy to thin tip to which can be tied an additional tip of even lighter weight to which the tiny fly is then tied. This taper is also a matter of balance, so that the whole rig handles in the air properly, casting the fly along for the ride. The proper combination can be tested for casting without a fly on the end, so you can see that it is not a matter of casting a weight, as is the case in bait casting or spinning.

The reel is of single-action type, that is, nonmultiplying as with spinning- and bait-casting types. In most light fly work, the fish is seldom played from the reel, but when playing big fish such as the bonefish or the Atlantic salmon the reel is used directly so that the line can go out freely without intervention by the hands. Ordinarily the reel is merely something to hold the line, which is stripped from it by hand or wound back on it when not needed.

The various types of flies used in fly fishing vary from the small wets, which are imitations of drowned or hatching aquatic insects upon which the trout and panfish feed. Nymphs are specially tied artificial flies made to more closely imitate the aquatic stages of the mayflies, caddis, and stone flies, principal food of the trout.

The long slim bucktail and streamer flies are designed to look like minnows and are used in trout, bass, and salt water angling. The big bushy bugs are for surface casting for bass in lakes and streams. Light hooks with very light leads are used with the fly rod for worm and live bait fishing.

Spinning tackle is a middle-of-the-road choice between fly- and bait-casting equipment. The rod is usually not as long as the fly rod but longer than the conventional bait-casting rod. The reason it is so long and limber is that it is used to throw light lures which are heavier than flies but lighter than regulation bait-casting plugs and spoons. The spinning rod, made either from split bamboo or tubular glass, is lined with very large-holed guides for the reason that the line peels off the rim of the spool, rather than straight out as in the case of the single-action fly or bait-casting reel.

The line used is braided nylon or monofilament, the latter being preferred by most anglers because it sinks better and does not have the tendency to fray and wear. It also has a certain amount of stretch that can mean the difference sometimes between a lost or creeled fish.

The reel has a stationary spool from which the line unwinds as demanded by the power of the cast. Thus it cannot

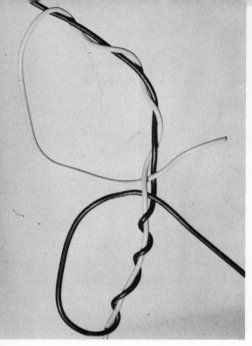

Start of the leader knot used to join two pieces of leader together.

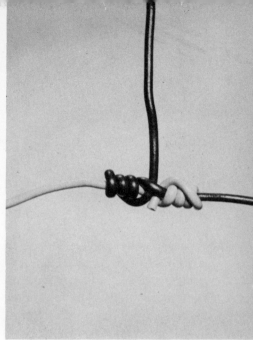

Finish of knot leaving one end for a tippet to use with extry fly.

Two knots for attaching hook.

Leader (white) attached to fly line. Tighten and it is solid.

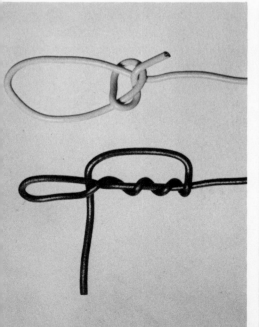

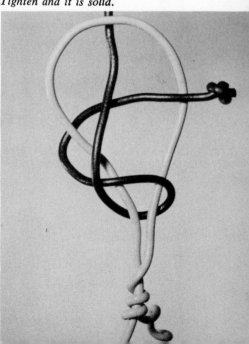

Salt water jigs are used for deep casting and trolling in fresh water for bass and big trout.

backlash or revolve over itself causing a tangle. The capacity of the average spinning reel is more than enough for the longest casts and hardest running fish. The reel is equipped with a built-in quickly adjustable drag and an anti-reverse mechanism which disconnects the handle when the line is being pulled out so that the handle does not revolve and slap your knuckles.

Spinning lures vary from ultralight little spinners, spoons, and plugs to the heavier types which can also be cast with light bait-casting rigs, so here you buy for both outfits when it comes to terminal tackle. This includes sinkers, bobbers, and hooks as well. Making your own flies and lures is great fun. The basic fly-tying equipment is illustrated on the opposite page.

Spin-casting equipment in the light and medium class is used for every species of fish in America except in Atlantic salmon fishing where it is not allowed. Your fresh water medium-sized outfit suffices for much light salt water fishing as well.

Typical bass bugs for surface fly-fishing for bass.

A selection of dry flies for trout.

A selection of nymphs which are fished deep for trout.

Bait-casting equipment is older in design than spinning gear but it is still irreplaceable in the opinion of many anglers. The shorter, stiffer rod with its smaller guides casts medium and heavyweight lures and baits with great accuracy. The rod is generally from four to five and a half feet long, fairly stiff, made of steel, glass, or split bamboo. The line is braided nylon to which is attached a short piece of leader, wire or monofilament, depending on the conditions.

There is more of a trick in handling the bait-casting outfit, for backlash can happen readily unless you learn to thumb the reel, that is, control the revolving spool as the cast is made. Too much pressure and you snub the cast, too little and the spool will overspin causing a tangle. A little practice will show you the right tensions which can also be adjusted by the pressure caps on the faces of the reel.

The big advantage of the bait-casting rod is that it is much more practical for deep-water trolling. It is also much more responsive for a quick strike to a heavy fish, especially if you have to strike against a bobber or heavy plug. The bait-casting rig had its start as the traditional outfit for bass fishing with plugs and spoons. It is used also for the bigger species of fish such as the pike and musky. In light salt water fishing it is tops when a quick fast strike is necessary and where generally heavier lures are used.

There are many types of rod action. Rod handles vary also, the offset handle being very popular today for it places the reel spool in a much better position for thumbing the line on the cast. Some reels are equipped with a star drag adjustment which makes it possible to change the pressure quickly even while playing a fish. This is borrowed from the salt water reels which have had star drags for many years.

Briefly this is the description of all three kinds of tackle used in fresh water fishing. Each, you can see, has its place. All can offer great fun with fish of all sizes.

The spinning outfit is the easiest to master as far as handling and casting are concerned, and its design allows a great overlap in both directions, toward the fly-rod lures of small size and toward the bait-casting lures of heavier duty. You can buy very strong spinning rods, so it behooves you to try spinning first unless your fishing will be exclusively for trout in small streams where a fly rod is really the best outfit.

Chapter IV

Fly Casting

The expert fly caster is an artist. He is also the epitome of a smoothly functioning combination of body and mind. More of the delicate touch is needed in fly casting than in other forms of casting, not that they do not require precision and a sense of timing, but fly fishing requires all these and more.

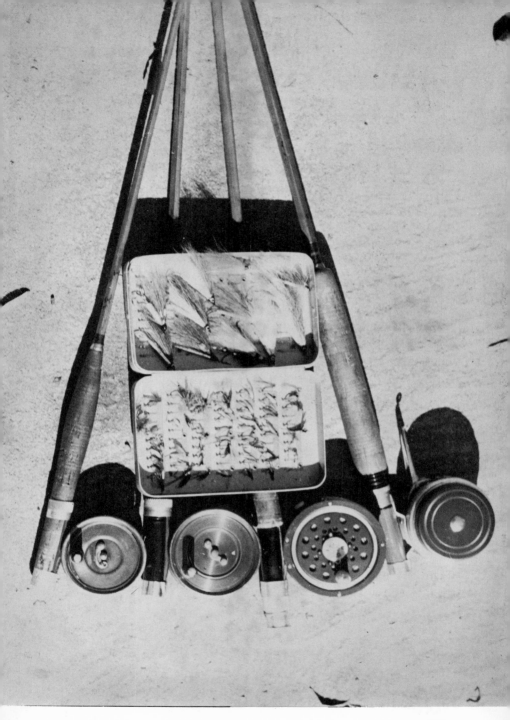

About a hundred years ago when fly fishing had its beginning in England and Europe the rods were long and flimsy. Trout tackle often reached a length of ten and twelve feet. Tackle was even longer for salmon. These rods were heavy and a heavy tapered line was required to cast the fly well out from the angler. It was a pretty problem to have the artificial fly merely alight on the surface and have it remain cocked in the upright position until a trout grabbed it.

Today, the modern angler has wonderful fly-fishing tools to work with. The modern rod has all the action needed. Lines are much more supple and float better. Leaders are much finer and stronger. Flies are tied much better.

The basic technique of fly fishing is really simple if you can remember a few basic points. Apply them and you will have no trouble.

The first is that you must make the rod do all the work. It does no good to merely wave the trout rod through the air and expect the line to straighten out or do what it is supposed to do in a specific cast. The whole trick is putting your mind to work so that all concentration is on the last two feet of the rod. This is the section which whips the line back and forth. The only way it can do its job is by pressure from below. In fly fishing the reel is located below the hand on the handle and acts as a sort of counterweight to balance the rod in your hand. The grip can either have the thumb placed on top of the rod or bent over the side of the cork handle. The first is recommended, although during a day of fishing it is often restful to vary the position.

The wrist does all the basic work in the cast. The action of the wrist is transformed through the rod and forces the rod to bend, thus pulling the line behind it. The more the rod bends in one direction, the more it will bend in the opposite. The more it bends from this initial human drive, the better and longer the cast will be. The whole arm, shoulder, and body are used for extremely long casts, but the center of action is still the wrist. Everything depends on this center of power. The wrist and its motion forms the basic fulcrum of power. Misuse

of the arm and incorrect synchronization will destroy the fulcrum.

Now, in order to make the rod cast the line out in front of you in the conventional fore and aft cast, the line must go an equal distance behind you. To go straight out to the desired distance, it must then go behind you the same length. This means that the same action of the wrist is needed to work in both directions in a smooth, synchronized movement.

To start, place the reel on the rod handle for either right- or left-hand winding, whichever is more comfortable. If you cast with the right hand and prefer to reel with the right hand this is correct except that it requires a shift each time you need to reel in line, especially when playing a fish. The hand that reels will also be used to strip line in and feed it to the rod as needed. The line should come out from the reel from behind the cross bar to be fed through the guides. The leader is attached to the line. The fly is tied to a tippet which is added to the tapered leader.

Proper way to grip the fly rod.

Strip line from reel and swing rod back.

Swing rod forward and control fall of line with line hand.

For powerful cast, draw line hard, bring rod back hard.

As rod comes forward, allow line to shoot through the fingers.

Now, we are ready. Strip off about fifteen feet of line from the rod tip and lay it on the ground in front of you. Grasp the free line between the reel and the first line guide, raise the rod tip up to the vertical position with a little snap of the wrist. Note that the line flips up and out behind you, the same distance in back as it was in front. Now, start again with the line in front, strip off another ten feet and back away from the line to take up the distance. Now, holding the spare line in the left hand, kick your wrist up and just before the line straightens out behind, kick it forward again. As the line straightens out in front of you, kick it back again before it drops to the ground and the line will go behind as it did on the first back throw. Keep on doing this and note that when you begin to wave the rod instead of kicking it with the wrist, forcing it to do the job, the line begins to fall sloppily. This means that you definitely have not snapped the wrist enough. If you find that you are snapping it too much, use a little less power. Do not wave the rod. Remember the fulcrum point and let all power come from there only.

Now, while you are casting the line in the air back and forth, strip out a half-arm's length of line from the reel and as the cast goes forward, release a little at a time. Release a little as the cast goes back. As the line lengthens in the air you will have to lengthen your timing on the forward and backward kick. Strip more line and feed it to the rod on the back and forward cast. Note the change in timing. Also note that now you will have to exert a little more power into the kicking action of the wrist. Practice the foregoing a few times to get the "feel" of the tackle in operation. Note that brute strength does not make the cast go any farther or land with more accuracy. When the rod is allowed to do its job, the angler merely directs and supplies the energy for the rod to work with.

To lay the cast down on the water, now that you have mastered the art of falsecasting in the air, you merely stop the rod on the forward throw and the line will lay itself out straight before you. When a lot of line is out, it is now necessary to strip in a couple of arms' lengths of line and hold them in coils in your left hand. It may seem awkward at first, but you'll soon get the hang of it. Strip in three coils of line and your initial casting line will be easy to cast back and forth in the false cast. To plan your casting direction, falsecast in the air, gradually moving into the direction desired; and when you have continued to release line and the cast is stretching out to the desired length, simply let it go.

To make really long casts, the double haul is used. Don't try this until you have mastered the simple fore and aft cast. The double haul adds resistance to the line on the pickup from the water in front of you and also heightens the pressure on the rod as you begin the forward cast. Strip line on the pickup to begin the pressure, and then strip again as you begin the forward swing. That is all there is to it.

To lay the line around a rock or snag where a curved cast is required, turn your wrist right or left and aid the action with a downward throw of the forearm. The line will shoot out as usual but will land with a curve in it of the desired degree. This one takes a little finesse, but you'll catch on to it quickly.

Be careful in all casting to keep the rod pointing almost straight up all the time. Work in a wedge shape in the air from a 10 o'clock to 2 o'clock direction as on your watch. This will insure your working the rod and not waving it. If you drop the rod down too far, particularly on the back cast, the forward cast will fall in a bunch. Don't wave the rod, kick with a generous snap of the wrist only. Think near the rod tip and make it work for you.

To execute the roll cast, one which is needed where there is no room for the back cast, start with the line out on the water. Point the rod across the stream, bring the rod to the vertical only and as the line comes back toward you, snap the rod forward and down to the lateral position again. You will see the line roll back in the air toward you and then go shooting out in front to fall where it came from. The action of the rod must be increased as the line is lengthened. This cast comes in mighty handy when your back is up against a bridge, a cliff, rocks, or overhanging brush. It is a graceful cast to watch and great to perform. It is often used in a wind when the fore and aft cast is impractical.

Line is cast adrift on the water.

When the fish strikes, the angler snaps the rod against him.

The roll-and-mend cast is simply the roll with either a right or left twist of the wrist and arm. This causes the line to roll back and then as the forward action is applied the wrist and the forearm from the elbow it causes the rod to swing directly in the right or left direction. The line rolls back and up and as it goes forward it flips a few feet in the direction desired. This cast, pictured at the front of this chapter, is used when you are fishing upstream and wish to make the next cast above the last one.

With these two casts well learned and under control you should soon be able to handle at least a forty-foot cast with exacting control. Do not attempt to cast further before this much line is mastered. Most of your fishing will be done within forty feet, so make sure you learn perfect control.

You will discover that the timing of the casts will have to be varied with the length of line in use and that the left hand, controlling the supply of line, can be used to quickly shorten or lengthen the line. A modified double haul will add the last-second timing of zest needed to direct the line in the air. You must gradually use your forearm to raise the whole cast higher from the water. At times the cast may be done with the arm extended straight up over your head.

Do not impair the action of the rod by any of this. Keep that fulcrum action.

One of the variations of the fore and aft cast is the side cast where you have to get the line to sail out under an overhang. Instead of casting up in the air, turn the rod parallel to the water and execute the cast close to the water. The roll cast can be used in the same way.

When fishing downstream and you wish to drop the fly near to your feet for a longer drift than is usual with a good straight-out cast, stop the action of the rod at vertical midpoint. The line will stop in the air, pull the fly back so that it lands almost under the tip of the rod. The drift will take up the slack and the fly will have fished the stretch of water in front of you.

As in tennis, the fore and aft cast can be executed by holding the rod across your chest and to the left so that you can fish the left bank of the stream.

Watch a good angler on the stream and study the way he casts. If he is a really good caster you will note that his motion is a symphony of perfect, effortless timing. He is hardly doing any work at all, for the rod is being used to its best. That again, is the entire secret.

Once these casts are mastered to a degree that you can go astream and put the flies about where you want them

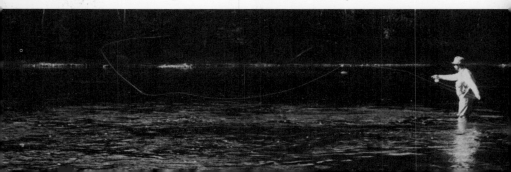

under any and all conditions, the choice of fly and specific technique is next on the list.

In stream fishing for trout, three types of flies are used. The heaviest and biggest flies are the streamers, made with chicken-neck hackle feathers, and bucktails, made from the tail hairs of a buck or doe deer. These last two types imitate the stream minnows upon which the trout feed. Being generally heavier than either wet or dry flies, they are tied to leaders with terminal test of not less than 3X designations. A leader that is too light will have a tendency to snap off on the cast or handle badly in the air on delivery. They are cast across and downstream with a twitching motion given them during their drift to simulate the movement of minnows trying to escape from the hungry trout. They are fished on the surface in clear water and allowed to go deeper in still or cloudy water. They are very effective as early season flies and big fish can be taken on them when other types fail to provoke a rise.

Wet flies are small, the size of the average underwater insect or a fly that has become a victim of the current. Most of them are less than an inch in length and tied very sparsely so they will sink readily in the current. Conventionally, wet-fly fishing is done in across-stream casts and the flies are allowed to drift straight down stream and then retrieved in skips and short jumps on or near the surface. At other times, when the water is calm and clear, they are allowed to simply drift at will in the current. Since the strike of the fish will not be felt if there is too much slack line, it behooves the angler to try to control the slack and develop sharp eyesight. Fish that hook themselves are lucky catches. The expert knows instinctively when to strike just at the time he sees the flash of a fish taking the lure.

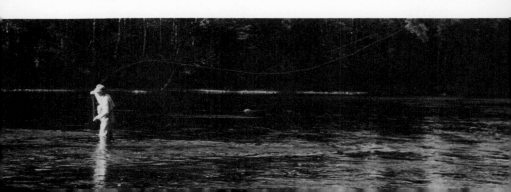

Nymphs are merely variations of wet flies and the technique for working them is about the same. The advantage of the nymph is that it looks to the trout like an underwater nymph, or water stage of the flying insects upon which the trout feed most of the time. Nymphs are made to sink readily and the deeper the better in the early season.

Dry flies are artificial lures made to represent the flying stage of the aquatic insects and also insects which have found their way to the stream from land. They are cast to be landed daintily on the water to imitate the live insect as best they can. As in all flies, the size, shape, color, and general behavior of the fly on the water spells the difference between a rise and a shunning from the trout. More finesse in the cast and a more stealthy approach to the area are needed when the fish are seen feeding on the insects that are alighting on the surface. Trout are very easy to scare with any false or sudden movements. Dry flies are cast up and across stream, or drop-stop cast downstream to drift from close to the rod tip to the extent of the line used. Use a fly dope to aid in floating.

In bass fishing, the streamer flies and the big fluffy bass bugs are used to great success particularly over touchy fish that are worked by many anglers. These lures are smaller than the spinning and bait-casting types and are not so apt to scare them. The typical bass-bug rod is longer and heavier than most used in trout fishing. The bass flies, being bigger and heavier and more wind resistant, demand a more powerful rod to get them out where they can do damage. Leaders and lines are also heavier to keep the balance.

In fly fishing for southern snook, tarpon, or bonefish, the heaviest and longest fly rod is none too much, for distance is the prime requirement. The best choice of rod for them is one that is used also in Atlantic-salmon angling—a rod of at least 9 feet and preferably 9½ to 10 feet. The double haul cast is almost always used in order to get as much distance as possible especially when casting into the wind.

You can let a big rod tire you out if you don't remember to let it work for you while you simply direct it with the wrist and the forearm motion. The relaxed shoulder and the pivot from the waist as in golf will help take the entire pressure off the wrist and so keep you from becoming overly fatigued.

Fly rods are used also for the smaller panfish found in fresh water. Given a light rod and some tiny flies, you can have a real day fishing for sunfish, crappie, or bluegills. Among the most sporty fish are the largemouth and smallmouth bass and rock bass that inhabit many warm-water, slow-moving rivers and streams. Use your trout flies on them, particularly the bucktails, and you'll be surprised at the fun they will offer.

In stream fishing other equipment needed includes a landing net that is attached to you by a stretching rubber cord. This can be dangled from across the shoulder. The fish is netted with the left hand while you hold the line in the rod hand under the index finger. Before you come to netting the fish, however, you must learn to strip in the line with the left hand and quickly switch to the right to reel in the slack line while still playing the fish. Sounds much more difficult than it really is.

The only law we set is to try not to horse the fish in or push your luck too hard. Get to know just how much pressure you can allow to the fish without breaking the leader by testing the leader. Either give the fish line or move toward him, or he will break the leader or pull the hook out. Too much slack line, however, will also let him get the upper hand and shake out the hook on a jump or sudden rush.

When you are ready to net the fish, don't swipe at it as if you were playing tennis. Place the major part of the net underwater and downstream from the fish. Lead the fish into the net and then scoop it up slowly. With the fish safely in the meshes you can then go to work getting the hook out. In order to keep the fish from thrashing, grab it behind the head and

squeeze. If the fish is small, take it by the lower lip, and bend down. This will paralyze the fish and it will stay still until you extricate the hook. Should the fish be too small to keep legally, or if you wish to return even a big fish, wet your hands before handling and above all be gentle. Extricate the hook as carefully as possible and gently place the fish back in the water holding it upright until it gets its wind. It will then live to fight another day.

Wading a trout stream, a fast mountain brook, or a mucky lake demands that you watch your step. Feel the bottom with your feet rather than walk as you would on dry land. Rubber boots are all right for average shallow-water fishing. But to angle the big river or the deep lake, waders should be used that are chest high with either boot feet of formed rubber or stocking feet over which are worn a pair of insulating wool socks and special wading shoes. In slimy rock streams or streams where the boulders are shiny smooth, a variety of accessory slip-ons such as felt or chain bottoms designed to grip under specific conditions are recommended.

Buy good tackle, get to know it, learn the ways of the current and you'll have fun fly fishing.

Chapter V

Bait Casting

The old reliable, the grand old standby, the bait-casting rig is an entirely different kind of casting and fishing combination.

Baits, that is heavy lures of the spinner, plug, or heavy bait type are shot out from the rod because of their weight. The rod is shorter than the fly or spinning rod and the reel has a revolving spool which has to be very well controlled. The reel is mounted on the top of the reel seat opposite the fly or spinning gear which hangs downward. The rod handle is either straight or offset for ease of casting and thumbing the reel. Mount the reel on the rod handle, thread the line through the level wind mechanism and then feed the line through the rod guides.

Attach a snap swivel to the end of the line and then snap on a practice plug without hooks. You are about to learn to cast, but before you begin, remember that the speed of the spools revolving must be adjusted properly to the weight of the lures being used. For the greatest distance, the tension adjustment caps on either side of the reel should be light. Control will be made with the thumb.

Let the practice plug hang down from the tip of the rod about six to eight inches. Grasping the rod in the right hand, place the thumb on the coil of line on the spool.

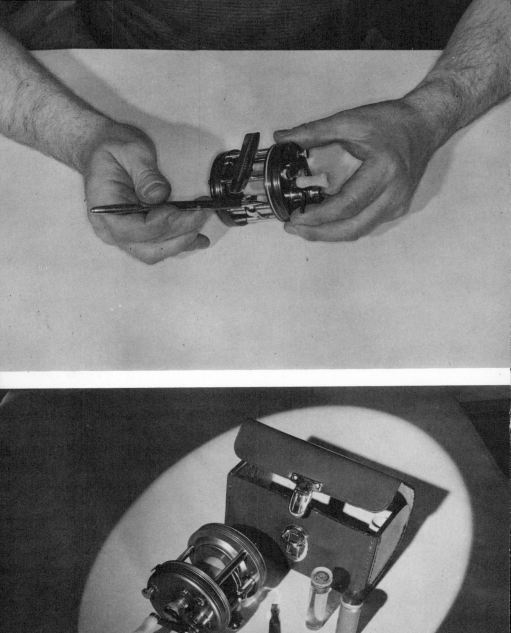

Selection of bass plugs from surface poppers to deep runners (should be in your tackle box).

By pressing the thumb on the line you can wave the rod back and forth a few times to get the feel of the rod's action. You will feel the plug pull on the rod as it swings in the air. Now, make the swing sideways from about 9 o'clock to 3 o'clock and at the end of the forward swing, release the pressure on the thumb to allow the plug to pull off line. It will shoot out from the rod in the direction of the rod tip. If you release it too soon, it will fly too far to the side and it will swing too far to the left of center. Try this a few times making very short casts until you perfect the timing of the thumb release. Now lengthen the cast by allowing freer spin of the reel spool and learn to stop it before it rolls over itself. The reason for this backlash is that the spool has revolved more than the demand of line has called for. It is up to you to control this.

Now you can get bold and try a longer cast, but before you make the first one, remember to control the line as you reel in so that it lies on the reel spool in steady tension. Unequal tension will cause the spool to revolve unevenly. To control this returning line, change the rod to the left hand, reeling with the right. With the thumb and forefinger, reach in front of the level wind bars and snub the line gently as you reel in with the right hand.

The sidewinder cast that you have been performing can now be perfected so that the line goes precisely where you want it to go. The next trick is to master all these operations so that they become almost automatic, for your attention should be on the fish that is out there waiting for your lure.

The overhand cast is step two and is a variation of just what you have been doing thus far, with the exception that it is much more accurate. Instead of casting to the side, you raise the rod straight up in front of you, so that the back and forward cast sights between your eyes. Now you can sight your cast and with the release controlled you can now begin to learn to stop the fly of the plug as it speeds its way toward the target.

With a little practice you should be able to hit a dinner plate at fifty feet. Remember to always snub in the line on the retrieve and you will have no trouble with backlash. Here, as in fly and spin casting, it is not brute force that makes a long cast. The cast is only as good as the rod and the man who works his wrist properly. A little extra power can be exerted by a shove with the forearm, but without maintaining the fulcrum of the wrist snap all the power will be wasted.

The back cast can be executed by merely pointing the rod across your chest toward the left and whipping the rod in the cast. Think out there near the tip and make that part of the rod take the pay load.

In striking the fish, you will have to quickly snub the line and yank back on the rod to exert pressure which will set the hook. As the fish pulls, you let the line slip under your

Proper way to hold bait-casting rig.

Proper way to hold rig for line rewind. Line is fed through the fingers for even tension on the spool.

thumb. Switch to the other hand so you can reel in with your right hand, now snubbing the line with your left hand. Reel against the fish's pressure, and let the reel handle go spinning within your hand held loosely around it for control and instant availability to winding when the fish slackens his run.

When the fish comes to net, you may want to switch the rod to the right hand again, controlling the line slip with the right thumb and do the netting with the right hand. A boat net, that is a landing net with a long handle, is best. The stream net need not have a long handle for use in wading the stream.

It is often advisable to use a six- or eight-inch plastic-covered metal leader before the plug when fishing for big bass, especially in weed beds or rocks, as this part of the line gets a lot of wear. Plugs, spoons, and spinners in combination with bait, and bait imitations are used in bass fishing as well as for pickerel, pike, musky, and the usual lake fishing, whether it be casting or trolling. Live-bait rigs merely involve the use of a sinker put on either before or after the nylon-snelled hook. For casting it is far better to have the weight on the very end.

When you wish to cast a piece of live bait with no weight, such as nightcrawlers, this can be done by merely tying on a leader-snelled hook to the end of the line. The cast must be very delicate and unless a very long and light-action rod is used, not too much distance can be had.

Trolling with bait-casting gear is one of its best uses. This is where the click is used best. On the side of some reels is a little lever or push button which will offer just enough tension on the reel to keep it from allowing the spool to revolve and so let out line. This lets you place the rod down in the boat while you are paddling. It is also used as a partial drag when playing the fish. Makes a very good alarm clock by the way!

The technique of bass fishing can be summed up very easily in basic principles. The learning will have to come from experience. Bass take anything that looks like food and under-

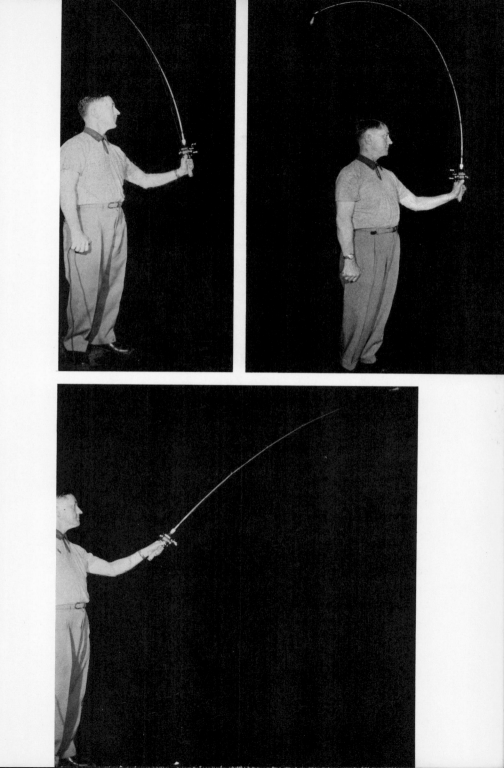

Various sinkers, bobbers, snap swivels and hooks comprise the bait-fishing (terminal tackle).

water and surface plugs are made to wobble, dive, run fast, and perform many kinds of contortions in order to attract any fish in the area. Color means a great deal, even though it is said that fish cannot distinguish color. We do know that they do see contrast and so plugs with contrasting colorations will look to them like wounded fish, frogs, or some other food.

In shallow-water fishing where you will encounter underwater snags, rocks, and weeds a weedless plug is the right medicine, and one which will not sink fast. Surface-popping plugs and plugs that dive down deeper as you retrieve faster can be used also. Retrieve very slowly in the shallows and faster as the water becomes deeper. Spoons and the spinning type of lure must be retrieved as soon as they hit the water to keep from sinking too fast.

The sidewinder cast or the overhead cast can be used. It is best, if you are fishing from a boat with a partner, to use the vertical cast unless you are working from one end of the boat and your cast is on your outside from the partner. In this way, it is impossible accidentally to hook him with a flying plug, or smash him in the face when by accident the plug pulls away from you on the swing because of a lack of thumb control on the line. Bass plugs with their treble hooks are nasty things to get caught up with, so be careful.

Bait fishing with this tackle can be done by still fishing —simply letting the line overboard, off the dock, or lightly cast into the water. Other types of bait fishing involve a long cast of the rig and allowing the bait to rest on the bottom. In this case, a slip sinker is used. Before tying on a hook, place a sinker with a hole through it to a stretch of the line so that when the fish picks up the bait, the weight will not be felt by the fish. If he feels this extra weight he might become afraid and drop it. The slip sinker does away with this possibility.

Great accuracy can be possible with this tackle and you will need it especially when spot casting to the edge of weed beds or lily pads. If fishing from the boat, try to judge the distance to shore by making a short practice cast, then by regulating the power of the cast with the thumb, you can stop the lure in midair and drop it precisely where you want it. Bounce the plugs off logs or rocks. This sends the bass crazy, for they think that the lure is some form of life that has fallen in the water.

You will discover that one rod will not be sufficient for all purposes. Sometimes a lighter rod will be necessary, at other times, particularly when trolling, a stiffer and shorter rod is used. A good reel with good line is a must. As in all methods, best tackle is the prime requisite. You cannot be a good bait caster without the best gear you can afford. Take good care of your tackle and there is no reason for it ever to wear out. The bait-casting reel needs frequent cleaning and oiling to keep it in tip-top shape. Bait casting can be fun when you know your tackle and just what it will do. Experiment with various weights of line in relation to the lures you use. Practice for accuracy in direction and distance and you will be able to hold your own with the experts.

Chapter VI

Spinning

This is the fishing method that is a halfway measure between fly and bait casting, but does not eliminate either. Fundamentally spinning is designed to throw lighter lures than bait-casting gear, and heavier lures than the fly rod. Ultralight spinning gear comes very near fly-casting gear, but does not

supplant it because a fly rod is the only rig with which you can successfully cast the dainty dry or wet lures and nymph flies.

Spinning gear also delivers very lightweight baits such as small red worms that are so deadly for trout. It is perfect for small live minnows.

Spinning rods come in a variety of weights and lengths in both glass and split bamboo. Some are long with light, wavy action, others are a bit shorter and stiffer, and then there are the rods built for heavier action that are both longer and harder. The ultralight rods are very short, under six feet, and have extremely soft action.

Spinning reels for fresh water are divided into two main classes, and include the ultralight reels with very small spools and the so-called standard size which varies a little before reaching into the medium and heavy weights used in salt water surf and deep sea fishing. It is best to start out with a medium-weight reel. A medium-weight rod for this will accommodate most of the spinners, spoons, and lures expressly designed for freshwater spinning. Many of the conventional bass plugs and lures used in bait casting have been made in lighter weights for spinning and they are no less deadly than their counterparts.

Live-bait rigs such as the conventional slip-sinker rig using a sinker with a hole through it to slip along the bottom as the fish grabs the bait, the usual sinker-at-the-end rig with the hook tied in above on a long snell, and the trolling rig where the bait is trailed behind a sinker and a fin to keep it from revolving—all these are applicable to spinning as well as bait casting and to a very small degree used with a stout fly rod.

Casting with the spinning outfit employs the same techniques as bait casting with the big exception being that it is not necessary to thumb the spool. A built-in drag which is quickly adjustable takes care of the fish's rush and the anti-reverse makes it unnecessary to stop the pull of the line by grabbing the revolving handle.

Here, as in bait casting, the timing of the line release on the cast is of the utmost importance in order to have the cast shoot out straight to or above the target area with a minimum of slack line drifting down on the water. It is often during the time of trying to reel in the extra slack due to a bad cast that a fish will hit and be missed because of the slack. A bit of practice and this will be mastered in the sidewinder as well as the vertical cast.

The one important advantage of spinning gear is that you can have one reel do the work of three, because of the interchangeable spools. For light work you can have one loaded with four-pound line, another with eight and still another with ten- or twelve-pound line.

Adjust the drag for line strength.

Test it.

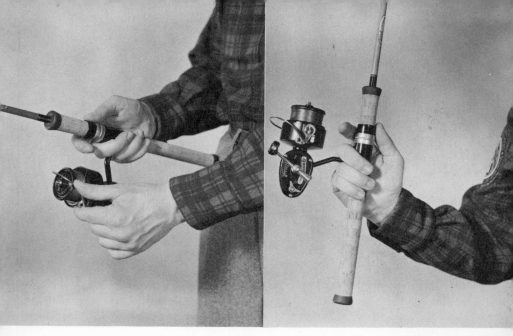

Grasp line in index finger and open bale.

Top of cast, line is still held firmly in trigger finger.

Swing rod forward easily on cast and release line from finger (for the cast).

The rewind of the line closes the bale.

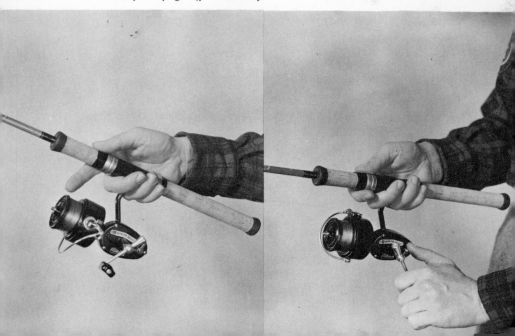

Closed face spinning reels.

The last two will not cast as well but are perfect for trolling or close-in bait fishing where big fish or snags are concerned. If you learn to change your reel spools when you change lure weights, you'll be operating at top efficiency. Casting a heavy lure with a very light line will lose many lures. A light lure cast on a heavy line will not go as far, nor will it act as well in the water as a lure of the proper weight. It is imperative that you attach a snap swivel to the monofilament line. Do not tie the lures directly as the line will tend to wear and break off. Short plastic-covered wire leaders should be used in rough areas or for big fish.

Open faced spinning reels.

You will note that spinning tackle lets you cast great distances. This is an allure that should not be overworked. The best fisherman is the one who can cast accurately and judge the water carefully rather than cast all over the water without serious intent. Just because you can cast across a wide trout stream does not mean that you will be able to control the flow of the lure in the water at that distance. It is more advisable to work the water area near you first, placing the lure in many combinations of ways across an area where the fish are lying. In this way, one of the angles can pay off in a strike. Do not cast too fast over a given spot. Let the area rest. Beating it to a pulp will tend to scare the fish. Also, it is known that fish will tire very quickly of seeing one type of lure swimming past them. Change your lures every couple of casts. One of them will be bound to tempt a fish if they act at all lifelike. Working a lure too fast in the water is another common fault. If a fish sees a fast-moving lure and doesn't get a chance at it, he will probably pass it up, whereas a slow-moving lure will be taken. In trout-stream angling, it is often effective to cast the lure upstream and reel in fast as the lure comes down toward you. In this way it has a chance to sink faster.

Assortment of light and medium all-purpose spinning lures.

Live-bait fishing with spinning gear is very effective. Hook on the baits but remember to cast them very lightly. If the stream is not too fast you can use unweighted minnows or worms and you'll find that when they drift naturally in the current you will get more strikes. The trick here is to allow just enough slack line, but at the same time do not allow too much line or you will not feel the hit. If you work with weighted bait, gradually start adding either split shot or wraparound lead to the leader well above the bait until a heavy enough rig is found to accommodate the casting distance. With the added weight, be careful to swing the cast easily or you are liable to flip off the bait in the air. Often it is best, if you intend to keep a live minnow live, to merely drop the minnow at your feet and let the current carry it down as you guide its course with the rod tip. Here again, try upstream casting and even the unweighted live minnow will have a chance to sink to the proper level.

There is a trick to properly setting the drag on the spool. Make sure you set it at below the breaking strain of the line. That initial hit of a fish can be quite sharp and sudden and if the drag does not let go instantly and smoothly, the line will break. It is best to test this out ahead of time and then label your spools.

Too many anglers lose too many lures in spinning. This should not be. The reason is that the proper lure designed to fit the specific situation is not used. A heavy spoon used in shallow water will tend to hit bottom before you have begun the retrieve that will keep it moving upward. Often if you hold the rod high you can avoid this, but it is much simpler to select a lighter lure. In current that is strong do not use a revolving blade spinner for it will pull much too hard and the strike of a fish will tend to break the line. Use a little common sense in lure selection and you should have no trouble with lost lures.

Weighted flies, particularly bucktails, are killers on trout and bass in streams and lakes, for they imitate the minnows upon which these fish feed. Another way of effectively using bucktail and streamer flies is to attach a weight up the line about two feet from the lure. Attaching it below the fly will tend to tangle the rig on the cast. Hold the rod high when fishing in shallow water and on the stream cast the flies slightly up and across, fishing them quite a way downstream before retrieving for a recast.

Since spinning started in this country about twenty years ago it has become very popular with fresh water and salt water anglers. It has been found the easiest of the three methods to master, especially in the casting and fishing part of it. More big fish have been taken on spinning gear than by other methods. But tackle isn't everything. Your judgment of line weight, type of lure, and general stream and lake knowledge are important. Playing the fish with this delicate gear is an art also. Trying to horse a fish in before it is ready robs you of much fun and can also rob you of a prize.

When it comes to the time of netting, ease the fish in close, lighten up the drag—remember, the shorter the line from the fish to the rod tip, the less stretch there will be in the line and the more the effect on the drag. A sudden movement by the fish can break the light monofilament with a resounding snap. As in all fishing, ready the net and do not swipe at the fish as if you were playing tennis. Take it easy and enjoy the fish's actions right up to the last moment.

As soon as you can, buy an ultralight spinning outfit. This is really the sportiest kind of fishing and it will allow you to get the most fun from the little fish as well as a thrill of a life-time with the big ones. It stands to reason that if deep-sea spin fishermen can land marlin, sailfish, and other big fish on conventional spinning gear, ultralight gear can do a whale of a job on anything we have in fresh water. The secret of killing fish with this light tackle is to have very sharp hooks and to learn just how hard you can strike, even if the action of the rod is light and soft. Once the hook is set deep enough you have a good chance of landing the most powerful fish in fresh water. You have more than enough line on the reel to accommodate his longest and wildest runs. Fish ultralight for trout and bass, and you'll find no other combination of gear will give you as much of a thrill.

Chapte VII

Fishing Adventures

So far in this book we have been sticking close to important facts and techniques. In planning a fishing adventure, there is a great deal of dreaming and scheming, but facts must be adhered to and, most of all, the detail work of proper advance thinking can make the big difference between a thrilling trip and a complete bust. Forget some major part of your equipment and you are out of business. This isn't so serious when the adventure is not far from home, but it can be a mighty frustrating experience to find that you have left your terminal tackle at home or did not put a particular lure selection in the duffle.

Fishing, like any other sport, demands that you plan ahead. A few trips will bring this home with emphasis. First, start out with full equipment. Bring everything at first and you won't wish you had what remains on your table at home.

The second step is to learn all you can from books about the fishing area, the fish species, and the general conditions which exist in that water. There are many books and magazines which continually write about these places. One of the best information sources in the states is the conservation department publications which tell in exact detail all about the specific area you are interested in. Travel folders usually glow over the good points but yield little if any authentic information. It is best to know all you can ahead of the trip. What you learn on the spot will be helpful if you are properly equipped. There is a lot of fun anticipating a trip to some far-off locale.

The next consideration is that of your company on this trip. If it is you who is taking dad, then assume your responsibility for your own gear. Chances are that he will be borrowing from you from time to time. But don't let him bear the entire planning burden. If he is taking you, then be doubly sure you are all set in every detail. This will make for a wonderful time together out in the open. When you can take care of your every need, he will see that you are gaining that all-important sense of responsibility.

If you are going to fish with one of your pals, make sure that he is the kind of a fellow who will not become touchy if you catch all the fish and he does not. Do your best to see that his outfit is as complete as possible before setting out. He should learn as you have that to fish properly means bringing all that is necessary whether he is taking a trip to a neighboring pond or a long drive and camp-out at some wilderness area.

Chances are that if you take seriously all the details of your fishing gear you will not slough off the details of camping or simple meals in the open.

Depending on where you live, there is excellent fishing within a practical distance from your home town, be it a northern wilderness lake in the eastern United States where you will encounter brook trout, land-locked salmon or bass, to the far West where steelhead and salmon are the prize. In between is the area of the smallmouth bass, pike, musky, and walleye. Down South it may be the largemouth bass, pickerel, and other fresh water game fish.

Bring a camera along to record the incidents of the trip and especially the fish that are caught. Make sure to photo them next to the tackle and lures. Make your pictures full of action. Don't just settle for a straight picture of some guy holding up a dead fish.

Fishing will at times encourage all the sportsmanship you can muster. You will have to adhere to rules on the number and size of the fish taken, and obey the forest laws. There will be no one around to make sure except possibly a surprise visit from a warden. Fair play will come into operation when fishing with a buddy. Taking turns at hot spots will be the order of the day and sharing gear may be in order.

Self-control will be tested often. Right at the time the fish are rising, you may get a tangle, or lose something overboard. This will tax your patience. Many things about the woods will test your patience more than once. But, no matter what happens, you will come to realize that in the woods and on the waters you are under full sail and all by yourself. Upon you alone your fun and success depends. This in itself is a prime reason why outdoor life is so much fun and can offer so much toward your development as a sportsman and a man. In no other way are the lessons of life made so obvious.

Then there is the beauty and wonder of nature as it really is that confront you. The damp of dawn with its stillness and sweet cold, the heat of the day that makes you sweat under the sun, the hard driving rain that chills you to the bone, the gorgeous sunsets, the thrill of seeing a big fish feed in a magnificent jump, the thrill of a sharp tug on the rod, and the sensation of success when you slip the net under a lunker—this is the outdoors and you are the prime actor in the scene, unhelped, unaided by another.

Glossary

Anti-reverse   mechanism which allows line to be pulled from reel with handle remaining set.

Aquatic insects   those born in the stream or lake and hatched to return to lay eggs, such as stone flies, mayflies, caddis flies.

Backlash   line rolling over itself backwards due to reel spool over-spinning.

Bait fishing   fishing with bait such as worms, minnows.

Bait casting   a term used to describe the casting of plugs or lures which imitate bait fish.

Balanced tackle   tackle which balances well in hand and also that which, properly selected, performs to its ultimate.

Bass-bug rod   a staunch fly rod heavier than the usual trout weight to cast heavy bass flies and bug imitations long distances.

Billfish   ocean fish having a long pointed bill.

Boat net   landing net with a long handle for use from small boat or canoe.

Brackish water   fresh water mixed with salt water.

Bobber   a float tied to the line to keep the weighted bait at the correct water depth.

Charter boats   big yacht-size fishing boats to be rented for private use by the day or longer.

Chumline   a line or slick on the water formed from the dumping of dead fish chum to attract fish.

Click   the sound of the drag mechanism on reels to control line outgo.

Creel   willow basket or canvas bag that holds the caught fish.

Dorsal fin   the top fin on the back of the fish.

Drag   on reel, controls the line flow from the reel spool.

Flies, artificial   those made to represent insects and bait fish on which the game fish feed.

Game fish   designated fish species known for their gamy fighting qualities and also those under conservation-law protection.

Gear/tackle   fishing equipment and accessories.

Horsing fish   trying to bring in a fish before it is sufficiently tired—a good way to lose it!

Level wind mechanism   winds the line on the reel spool evenly
   without the aid of the guiding fingers of your hand.
Nonmultiplying reel   single action, that is one revolution of the
   spool to one of the handle.
Offset handle   handle with the reel seat offset for better positioning
   for ease in fishing.
Panfish   small fish that fit in the frying pan.
Practice plug   a rubber plug, similar in size and design as a fishing
   plug without hooks for practice casting.
School fish   fish that travel in bunches.
Single action reel   nonmultiplying.
Snap swivel   a swivel with a snap attached to it for attaching leaders,
   or additional terminal tackle or lures.
Stillfishing   fishing without moving from anchored boat on a lake
   or quiet stream. The bait is cast and allowed to stay there
   awaiting the fish.
Strip line   draw line from the reel for casting (fly fishing only).
Star drag   adjustable drag with hand mechanism designed to look
   like points of a star for easy and quick grasping.
Striking   pulling sharply on the line against the hit of a fish in order
   to set the hook in his mouth.
Tapered leaders   almost transparent leaders attached to the line and
   the end lure that taper from thick to thin in order to make
   the cast balance out in the air and float down on the water
   with minimum of disturbance (fly fishing only).
Tapered lines   lines tapered from thick to thin to balance the line in
   the air for best casting (fly fishing only).
Terminal tackle   that which is attached to the end of the line, leaders, spreaders, sinkers, hooks, bobbers, lures.
Thumbing the reel   controlling the outgo of the line by pressing on
   the spool during the cast (bait casting only).
Trolling   dragging the bait or lure behind a moving boat.
Ultralight tackle   the lightest and sportiest tackle practical for the
   fishing conditions and fish species.
X designation   the diameter and pound test of leader material and
   monofilament lines for spinning and bait casting.

Bibliography

Bates, Jr., Joseph D.: STREAMER FLY FISHING. New York, D. Van Nostrand Co., 1950.

Bergman, Ray: TROUT. New York, Alfred A. Knopf, 1959.

Brooks, Joe: COMPLETE BOOK OF FLY FISHING. New York, A. S. Barnes & Co., 1958.

Brown, Roderick Haig: FISHERMAN'S WINTER. New York, William Morrow & Co., 1954.

Bueno, Bill: AMERICAN FISHERMAN'S GUIDE. New York, Prentice-Hall, Inc., 1952.

Caine, Lou S.: NORTH AMERICAN FRESH WATER SPORT FISH. New York, A. S. Barnes & Co., 1949.

Camp, Raymond R.: FISHING THE SURF. Boston, Little, Brown & Co., 1950.

Cannon, Raymond: HOW TO FISH THE PACIFIC COAST. Menlo Park, Lane Publishing Co., 1956.

Evanoff, Vlad: SURF FISHING. New York, The Ronald Press Co., 1958.

Farrington, Jr., S. Kip: FISHING THE ATLANTIC. New York, Coward-McCann, Inc., 1949.

LaBranch, George M. L.: THE DRY FLY & FAST WATER. New York, Charles Scribner's Sons, 1914.

La Monte, Francesca: MARINE GAME FISHES OF THE WORLD. New York, Doubleday & Co., 1952.

McClane, A. J.: THE AMERICAN ANGLER. New York, Henry Holt & Co., 1951.

National Geographic Magazine: THE BOOK OF FISHES, 1952.

Quick, Jim: FISHING THE NYMPH. New York, The Ronald Press Co., 1960.

Ritz, Charles: A FLY FISHER'S LIFE. New York, Henry Holt & Co., 1959.

Rodman, O. H. P.: HANDBOOK OF SALT WATER FISHING. Philadelphia, J. B. Lippincott Co., 1952.

Wulff, Lee: ATLANTIC SALMON. New York. A. S. Barnes & Co., 1958.

Index

FRANK HOBBS